My Kwa Nzaa JOURNAL

A Year-long celebration

KWANZAA
FAMILY - COMMUNITY - CULTURE
DEC 26 - JAN 1

Self Determination
Cooperative Econimics
Creativity
Unity
Faith
Purpose
Collective Work and Responsibility

2 4 6 1 7 5 3

Special Edition

Sam and Rita Burke

BURKE'S PUBLISHING

Copyright 2025 by Sam & Rita Burke.

Publisher: Burke's Publishing
Author: Sam & Rita Burke

Published January 2025

ISBN: 978-1-998247-05-9
https://ILikeBeingMeBooks.com

Name_____

Journalist

In Swahili

JAMBO ➡ **MEANS** ➡ "HELLO."

KARIBU ➡ **MEANS** ➡ "WELCOME."

HABARI GANI ➡ **MEANS** ➡ "WHAT'S THE GOOD NEWS?"

Habari Gani

Unity

1

UMOJA – UNITY

When spider webs unite, they can tie up a lion

- African Proverb

Habari Gani

Self Determination

2

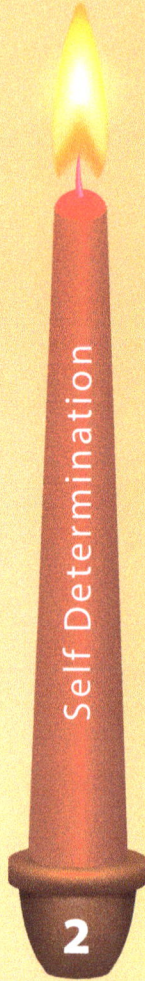

KUJICHAGULIA – SELF-DETERMINATION

There's always something to suggest that you'll never be who you wanted to be. Your choice is to take it or keep on moving.

– Phylicia Rashad

Habari Gani

Collective Work and Responsibility

3

UJIMA – COLLECTIVE WORK AND RESPONSIBILITY

Talent wins games, but teamwork and intelligence win championships

– Michael Jordan.

Habari Gani

Cooperative Economics

4

UJAMAA – COOPERATIVE ECONOMICS

Never ever chase money. You should chase success because, with success, money follows.

– Wilfred Emmanuel-Jones

Habari Gani

5

NIA – PURPOSE

Until all of us have made it, none of us have made it

— Rosemary Brown

Habari Gani

Creativity

6

KUUMBA – CREATIVITY

The most authentic thing about us is our capacity to create, to overcome, to endure, to transform, to love and to be greater than our suffering

– Ben Okri

Habari Gani

Faith

7

IMANI – FAITH

Faith is taking the first step even when you can't see the whole staircase

– Martin Luther King Jr

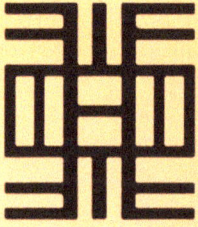

I AM

↓

Motivated

Inspired

Celebrated

Affirmed

I am deliberate and afraid of nothing.

— Audre Lorde

Reflections
From Me To We

• • •

In the spirit of our ancestors bold,
We will honour proven principles, forever to hold
With Kwanzaa's teachings as our guiding light,
illuminating the path through day and night.

• • •

Umoja - Unity

• • •

We will stand together as one strong family,
United in our quest for brighter days eventually
Supporting each other through trials and strife,
Together, we rise in the journey of life.

• • •

Confidence

Kujichagulia - Self-Determination

· · ·

We will define ourselves by our standards set high,
Unapologetically proud of our heritage, never to deny.
We will choose our path with intention and care,
And forge our destiny with courage and flair.

· · ·

Responsibility

Ujima
-
Collective Work and Responsibility

• • •

We will work together for the greater good,
Lifting each other as we strive and as we should.
We will share our knowledge, skills, and time,
Building a stronger community, one individual at a time.

• • •

Ujaama - Cooperative Economics

• • •

We will support each other's businesses and endeavours, too
Building thriving economies that benefit me and you.
We will invest in our communities with love and care,
As we create a brighter future for all to share.

• • •

Nia - Purpose

• • •

We will strive for excellence in all that we do,

Pursuing our passions with purpose anew.

We will stay focused on our goals with determination and might,

And celebrate our successes with much joy and delight.

• • •

Kuumba - Creativity

● ● ●

We will express ourselves through individual and collective creativity,

Celebrating our individuality with harmony and spirituality.

We will innovate and improvise with imagination and flair,

While bringing new ideas to life with courage and care.

● ● ●

Imani - Faith

• • •

We will trust in ourselves, our community, and our way,

Having faith in our abilities every single day.

We will believe in our resilience and our capacity to thrive,

And have confidence in our future, with hope always alive.

We will embody Kwanzaa principles every day of the year,

And strive to be the best version of ourselves with courage and flair.

• • •

When we embrace the Kwanzaa principles, we find our true strength. This will inspire our community to thrive through unity, which is in keeping with our collective purpose and intent.

I
LIKE
BEING
ME
BOOKS

Personal Promise

• • •

I will remind myself that tiny bits of progress lead to significant results. As Lewis Carroll says, I will guard against having regrets for the chances I didn't take, the relationships I was too afraid to have, and the decisions I waited too long to make.

• • •

Daily, we will embrace the seven Principles of Kwanzaa on these pages to maintain an Afri-centric perspective

Let's continue pulling together

(Harambee)

More Books By These Authors

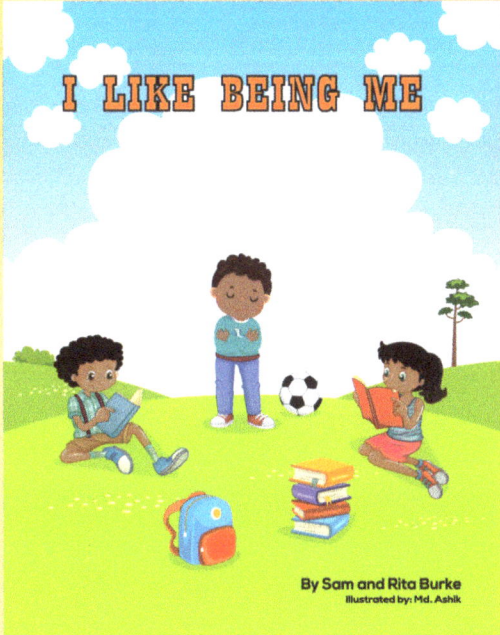
I LIKE BEING ME
By Sam and Rita Burke
Illustrated by: Md. Ashik

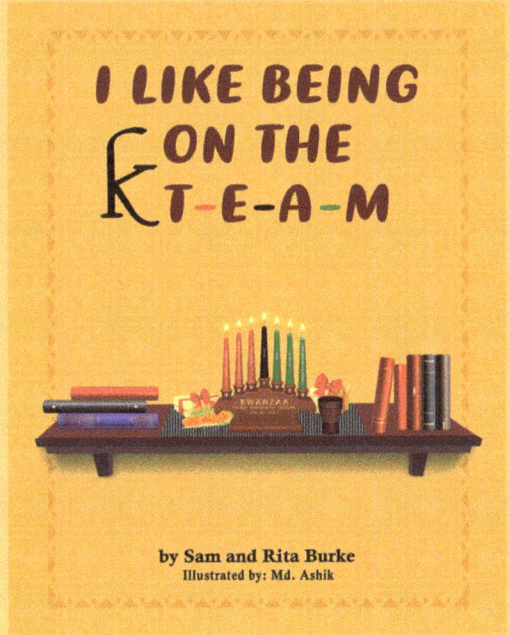
I LIKE BEING
KON THE
T-E-A-M
by Sam and Rita Burke
Illustrated by: Md. Ashik

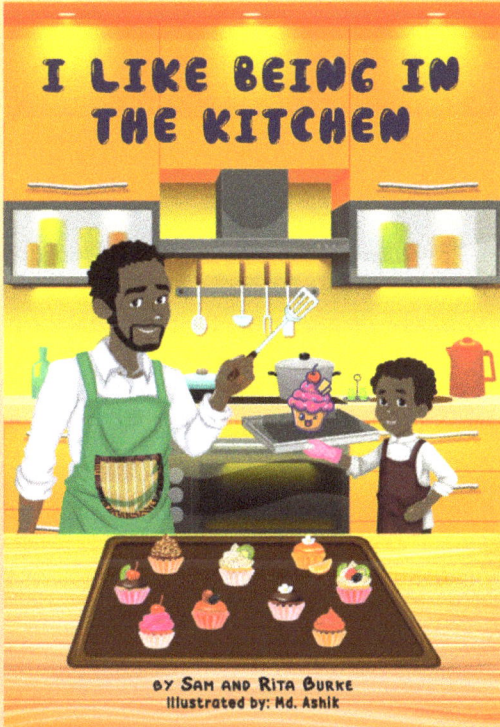
I LIKE BEING IN THE KITCHEN
BY SAM AND RITA BURKE
Illustrated by: Md. Ashik

Sam and Rita have been proudly celebrating Kwanzaa since 1995. They continue to do so annually by hosting a Global online Kwanzaa event which takes place December 27

For Books and Contact:
https://ILikebeingmeBooks.com